ELECTRICITY
AND MAGNETISM

YESTERDAY'S SCIENCE
TODAY'S TECHNOLOGY
SCIENCE ACTIVITIES

ELECTRICITY
AND MAGNETISM

ROBERT GARDNER

DRAWINGS BY DORIS ETTLINGER

TWENTY-FIRST CENTURY BOOKS

A DIVISION OF HENRY HOLT AND COMPANY / NEW YORK

Twenty-First Century Books
A Division of Henry Holt and Company, Inc.
115 West 18th Street
New York, NY 10011

Henry Holt® and colophon are trademarks of
Henry Holt and Company, Inc.
Publishers since 1866

Published in Canada by Fitzhenry & Whiteside Ltd.,
195 Allstate Parkway, Markham, Ontario L3R 2T8

Library of Congress Cataloging-in-Publication Data
Gardner, Robert, 1929–
Electricity and magnetism / Robert Gardner.
p.   cm.—(Yesterday's science, today's technology)
Includes index.
1. Electricity—Experiments—Juvenile literature.
2. Magnetism—Experiments—Juvenile literature.   [1. Electricity—Experiments.
2. Magnetism—Experiments.   3. Experiments.]
1. Title   II. Series: Gardner, Robert, 1929-
Yesterday's science, today's technology.
QC527.2.G38   1994
537'.078—dc20   93-40769
CIP
AC

ISBN 0-8050-2850-1
First edition—1994

Printed in Mexico
All first editions are printed on acid-free paper ∞.

1   3   5   7   9   10   8   6   4   2

Photo Credits

p. 29: © A. B. Joyce / Photo Researchers, Inc.; p. 37: © Kent Wood / Photo
Researchers, Inc.; p. 39: © Xerox Corporation; p. 50: © Johnson Controls, Inc.;
p. 56: © George Haling / Photo Researchers, Inc.; p. 65: © Westinghouse Electric
Corporation; p. 73: Department of Energy; p. 74: Department of Energy

CONTENTS

INTRODUCTION

To appreciate how important electricity is, think of what it would be like if you were suddenly shut off from all sources of electric energy. We are so dependent on electricity that it's difficult for us to realize that only a century ago gas or oil lamps and candles were used to light homes at night. Cooking was done on or in a wood or coal stove that was also used to heat water for dishes and baths. Clothes were washed by hand and dried on lines out-of-doors or over the stove. Buildings were heated with gas, coal, or wood stoves or furnaces, or with an open fireplace. Food was stored in iceboxes. A large block of ice at the top of the insulated box melted as it absorbed heat from food placed in the box. Periodically, an iceman delivered a fresh piece of ice and removed the meltwater that collected in a pan under the box. The blocks of ice were cut from lakes and ponds during the winter and stored under insulating layers of sawdust in tall icehouses with vents near the roof that allowed warm air to escape.

The phonograph, which had recently been invented by Thomas Edison, was powered by winding a spring. In most homes there was no electrical energy to operate light bulbs, to heat, pump, or circulate water, to power clothes washers or dryers, or to run the compressors in refrigerators or freezers. Radio, television, dishwashers, toasters, and computers, a few of the many items we take for granted today, had not been invented.

Today our entire way of life depends on electrical energy and the technology used to provide and distribute that energy. Giant generators convert the energy in steam or falling water into electric energy that is carried by metallic wires to millions of homes, schools, factories, and businesses. There the energy is used to illuminate space, turn engines, ignite furnaces, and power refrigerators and hundreds of other appliances that make our lives so much easier and diverse than those of our nineteenth and early twentieth century ancestors.

It was well into the twentieth century before technology made electrical energy available to much of America. But the science on which that technology was based was discovered early in the nineteenth century by such pioneers as Michael Faraday and Hans Christian Oersted.

In this book, you'll have an opportunity to investigate some of the science and technology associated with electricity. You'll learn, in hands-on fashion, how electrical energy can be generated and how electricity is related to magnetism. Because the generation of electric energy in modern power stations depends on magnetism, we'll begin by looking closely at magnets.

Each chapter contains a number of activities designed to enhance your understanding of the subject. You will find a ✖ beside a few of the activities. The ✖ indicates that you should ask an adult to help you because the activity may involve an action or the use of something that might be dangerous. Be sure to find adult help before attempting activities marked in this way.

Some of the activities, which are preceded by a ★, might be appropriate starting points for a science fair project. Bear in mind, however, that judges at such contests are looking for original ideas and creative thinking. Projects copied from a book are not likely to impress anyone. However, you may find that one or more of the activities in this book will stimulate a project or experiment of your own design that will lead you to the winner's circle at your school's next science or invention fair.

1

MAGNETS, COMPASSES, AND TECHNOLOGY

Some theorize that Chinese explorers invented the magnetic compass as early as 2300 B.C., but Thales, an early Greek philosopher, is believed to be the first person to investigate magnetism. Thales lived near the town of Magnesia, where shepherds found that their iron-tipped staffs seemed to "stick" to certain rocks. Thales obtained samples of these magnesian rocks and noted that they exerted strong attractive forces on all iron objects and on one another. Later, magnesian rocks came to be known as lodestone.

Early compasses were made by attaching a lodestone to a piece of floating wood. The lodestone, free to turn on the floating wood, always aligned itself in a north-south direction. (Lodestone, which means *leading stone*, is magnetite—a compound of iron and oxygen.)

By the eleventh century, people had discovered that a sliver of iron could be made magnetic by stroking it with lodestone. The iron sliver, or magnet, would line up in a north-south direction when suspended from a thread or allowed to float on a cork in water. The end of the magnet that pointed north was called the north pole of the magnet. The other end was the magnet's south pole. As ships began to venture beyond the sight of land, sailors carried lodestone on board. If an iron sliver (compass needle) lost its magnetism because someone dropped it, its direction-giving quality could be restored by stroking it with lodestone.

It was difficult to float a needle in a boat on rough seas, but by the sixteenth century dry, mounted compasses were in use. They were similar to the ones you may be familiar with, the ones used in scouting and in schools. European sailing vessels at this time mounted their dry compasses in supports that kept the compass in a horizontal position. These compasses are still used on ships, planes, and even in some automobiles. Hikers, climbers, and explorers also carry lightweight, dry-mounted compasses.

Compass Problems

When Columbus crossed the Atlantic in search of a new world, he noticed that the compass slowly changed its direction with respect to the stars. He kept this a secret from his crew for fear they would mutiny.

Today, we know that a compass does not point toward true north (the north pole) at all places on earth. If you live in Boston, a compass will point 15 degrees west of true north. In central Texas, it points 10 degrees east of true north. In Florida, it will point very nearly toward true north. The difference in angle between the compass reading and true north is known as the *magnetic declination*.

The problem is further complicated by the fact that magnetic declination changes with time. William Gilbert (1544–1603) found that in London his compass pointed 11 degrees east of true north. By 1657, a compass in London pointed true north. Today it points about 7 degrees west of north. However, the magnetic declination in London has been as much as 25 degrees west of north during the last 300 years. Gilbert also discovered that a compass not only pointed north, but it also turned downward (dipped). To explain the behavior of compasses, which are really small magnets, Gilbert suggested that the earth acts like a giant magnet.

The drawings in Figure 1a show the earth as a giant magnet and the changes in the location of one pole that have taken place over time. The arrows in the second drawing indicate the earth's magnetic field. A magnetic field gives the direction and strength of the magnetic force around the poles of a magnet. The direction of the field is the direction the north-seeking pole of a compass needle points. The strength of a field is given by the concentration of the lines. Where the lines are close together, the field is strong.

Figure 1b shows the angles of declination and dip at various places in the United States. Along each of the lines shown, the declinations are the same. The size of the declination is indicated on the lines.

Gilbert found, as you can, that the north poles of two magnets repel one another. Similarly, south poles repel. But the north pole of one magnet will attract the south pole of another. To determine which end of a magnet was its north pole, Gilbert simply suspended a magnet on a fine thread. The end that pointed north when the magnet stopped turning he called the north or, better, the north-seeking pole of the magnet.

Using Gilbert's definition, the earth's magnetic pole, which is found between Canada and the north pole, must be a south-seeking pole. Why?

 ACTIVITY 1

MAGNETIC FIELDS

MATERIALS
- *bar magnet*
- *magnetic compass*
- *iron filings*
- *tape*
- *sheets of white paper*
- *thin sheet of cardboard*

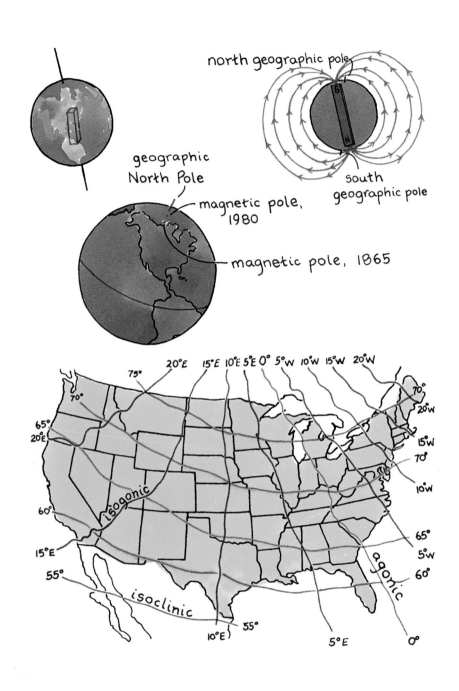

north geographic pole

south geographic pole

geographic North Pole

magnetic pole, 1980

magnetic pole, 1865

20°E 15°E 10°E 5°E 0° 5°W 10°W 15°W 20°W

75°

70°

65°

60°

55°

70°

65°

60°

55°

20°E

15°E

20°W

15°W

10°W

5°W

isogonic

agonic

isoclinic

10°E

5°E

0°

The magnetic field lines shown in Figure 2 can be mapped quite easily by moving a magnetic compass around a bar magnet. You'll see that the compass needle indicates a pattern very similar to the one shown in the drawing, but the compass needle is too long to reveal details in the pattern of the field. To get a better view of the field, you can use iron filings. These small pieces of iron are easily magnetized and behave like tiny compass needles.

You can get iron filings from your school science teacher or from a hobby shop, or you can make them from steel wool. To make them, you'll need a new pad of fine steel wool. Find the end of the roll and unroll it a few inches. To eliminate long stray fibers, trim the ends and sides of the roll with scissors. Then use the scissors to cut very narrow strips from the roll. Make the strips as narrow as you can so that the fibers will be very short. Let the tiny pieces of steel fall onto a sheet of paper. You can then use the sheet as a chute to empty the particles into an old salt or pepper shaker.

Tape a sheet of white paper to a thin sheet of cardboard. Place the cardboard on a strongly magnetized bar magnet, and sprinkle some iron filings on the paper. Tap the cardboard gently to free the filings so they become aligned like tiny compass needles in the field of the magnet. Does the pattern resemble the one shown in Figure 2?

Figure 1: a. The earth acts as if it were a giant magnet. b. A magnetic map of the conterminous United States showing the declination of a compass from true north and the angle of dip. The more or less vertical but irregular lines show positions of equal declination. They are called isogonic lines. On the map shown, the angles of declination vary from 20° W to 20° E. The agonic line shows the positions where a compass needle points toward true north. The irregular more or less horizontal lines are isoclinic lines. They show positions where the dip angles of a compass needle are equal. On the map shown, the dip angles vary from 55° to 75°.

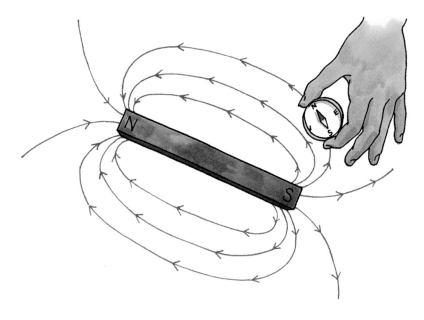

Figure 2. Some of the magnetic field lines around a bar magnet

WILL MAGNETS ACT
THROUGH OTHER MATTER?

MATERIALS
- *strong magnet*
- *tack*
- *paper clip*
- *wooden or plastic ruler*
- *glass jar*
- *pieces of paper, wood, plastic, rubber*
- *water*
- *various metals*
- *books*
- *tape*
- *thread*

- *coin*
- *"tin" can lid*
- *scissors*

A magnet will attract a steel tack or a paper clip. Will there be any attraction if you place a wooden or plastic ruler between the paper clip and the magnet? Carry out an experiment to find out.

If you place a tack inside a glass jar, can a magnet attract the tack through the glass? Can a magnet act through paper? Wood? Plastic? Rubber? Water? Metal?

Here's a fun thing to try. Use a pile of books to hold a bar magnet as shown in Figure 3. Then tie a paper clip to a fine thread. Tape the lower end of the thread to a table or the floor. The magnet should be strong enough to keep the paper clip suspended as shown in the drawing.

Knowing what a magnet will act through, see if you can predict what will happen if you slide a piece of paper or a plastic bag between the paper clip and the magnet. How about a coin? A "tin" can lid? Scissors?

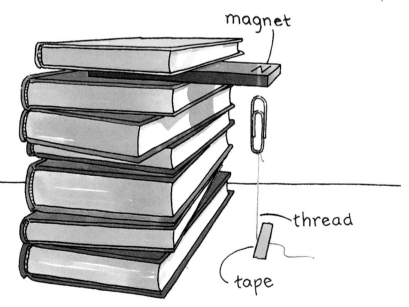

Figure 3. A magnet can make a paper clip "float" in air.

A MAGNET SUSPENDED
ABOVE THE EARTH

MATERIALS
- *various magnets*
- *thread*

Remember that a magnet "feels" the forces exerted by the earth's magnetic field. To observe this phenomenon, suspend several magnets by threads. Be sure the magnets are far from any metallic objects. When the magnets finally come to rest, you can see that they are all parallel to one another and aligned along a north-south line. Leave these magnets until you have completed the next experiment.

THE EFFECT OF A MAGNET
ON A COMPASS NEEDLE

MATERIALS
- *magnet*
- *magnetic compass*
- *suspended magnets from Activity 3*

Bring the north-seeking pole of a magnet slowly toward the north-seeking pole of a compass. Be careful not to bring the magnet so close to the compass that the compass needle spins wildly. What happens to the north-seeking pole of the compass as the north-seeking pole of the magnet is brought near it? What happens if you bring the south-seeking pole of the magnet slowly toward the north-seeking pole of the compass? If you bring the north-seeking pole of the magnet slowly toward the south-seeking pole of the compass?

You know that the north-seeking end of a magnet or compass needle always points in a northerly direction. What does that tell you about the kind of magnetic pole located high in the Northern Hemisphere? Is it a north-seeking or a south-seeking pole?

Take one of the suspended magnets used in Activity 3 and slowly bring the northernmost end of that magnet toward the north-seeking pole of the compass needle. Was that end of the suspended compass a north-seeking or south-seeking pole? How can you tell?

Test the other suspended magnets in the same way. Are the results the same?

★ **A C T I V I T Y 5**

MAKING A MAGNET
AND A COMPASS

MATERIALS
- *large sewing needle*
- *magnetic compass*
- *strong magnet*
- *thread*
- *water*
- *plastic container*
- *clay*
- *test tube*
- *long hat pin*
- *Ping-Pong ball*

To see how early Chinese or European navigators made compasses to guide them on their long journeys, you will need a large sewing needle. Hold the needle near a compass. There should be little or no effect on the compass needle. Now stroke the needle with a magnet as shown in Figure 4. Always stroke in the same direction. By so doing, the tiny atomic magnets within the needle will align themselves in the same direction. In this way, their magnetic effects can be made to add up instead of cancel one another.

Now bring the needle near the compass. What happens? (If you see no effect, try stroking another needle.) How can you tell which end of the needle is the north-seeking pole?

You can make your own compass and, at the same time, see water's skinlike surface. Place the needle on a sling made from thread and very gently place it on the surface of some water in a plastic container. (Be sure that both the water and container are very clean and free of any soap or detergent.)

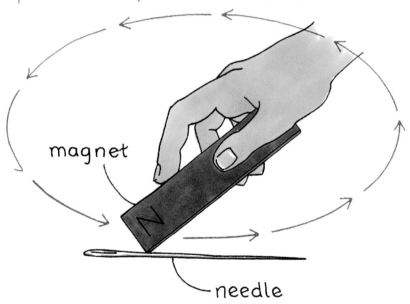

magnet

needle

Figure 4. A needle can be magnetized by stroking it with a magnet.

Which way does the north-seeking pole of your magnet point when it comes to rest?

You can also make a compass by magnetizing a needle (see Figure 4) and placing it on a tiny piece of clay that is fixed to a small inverted test tube. The test tube can then be balanced on a long hat pin as shown in Figure 5a. The base or head of the pin is supported by a large lump of clay placed far away from any metal objects. The test tube will rotate quite freely on the tip of the pin. When it finally comes to rest, in which direction does the needle point? How can you test to determine that it is the north-seeking pole of the magnet that points in a northerly direction?

Figure 5b shows still another way to make a compass. A Ping-Pong ball with a large lump of clay on its lower side is placed in a container of water. A tiny piece of clay on the top

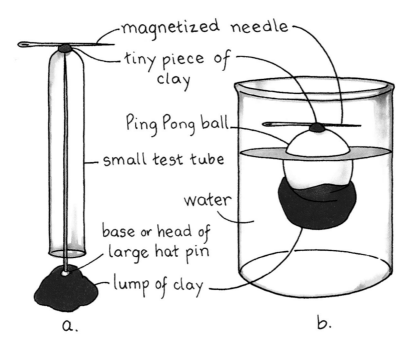

Figure 5. Two magnetic compasses that you can make

of the ball is used to support a magnetized needle. In which direction does the north-seeking pole of the needle point when it finally comes to rest?

✖ ACTIVITY 6

THE MAGNETIZING PROCESS

MATERIALS
- *paper or funnel*
- *small test tube or large, clear straw*
- *iron filings*
- *cork or clay*
- *strong magnet*
- *magnetic compass*
- *soft (gray cast) iron rod*
- *hammer*

Use a paper chute or a funnel to fill a small test tube or a large, clear soda straw sealed at one end about three-quarters full with iron filings. Use a cork to seal the test tube or clay to seal the ends of the straw. Stroke the tube or straw with a magnet as shown in Figure 4. What happens to the iron filings as you stroke the tube or straw?

Bring the test tube or straw near a compass. What evidence do you have that the test tube or straw has been turned into a magnet? Which end of the tube or straw is the north-seeking pole?

You can use the iron filings in the tube or straw to see how heating or dropping a magnet can cause it to lose its magnetism. Shake the straw or tube. Again, bring the tube or straw near a compass. What has happened to the magnet?

Here's a way to amaze your friends. Find a long soft (gray

cast) iron rod that has very little effect on a compass needle. (If it has an effect, turn it so it points in an east-west direction and drop it on the floor a few times. That should remove most of its magnetism.) Ask an adult to hold the rod so it is in a north-south direction with the north end tilted downward. The adult should then strike the rod sharply several times with a hammer. When you bring the rod near a compass needle, you will find that the rod has become a magnet. Can you explain why?

★ **ACTIVITY 7**

USING A COMPASS
TO ESTABLISH DIRECTION

MATERIALS
- *smooth square board about 30 cm (1 ft) on each side*
- *level surface such as a table or top of a wall*
- *tape*
- *paper*
- *magnetic compass*
- *pencil*
- *ruler*
- *protractor (optional)*

To see how a magnetic compass can be used to find the direction to an object, take such a compass outdoors. Place a smooth board on a level surface such as a picnic table. Tape a sheet of white paper to the board, and place a magnetic compass at its center. Use a pencil to mark the position of the north- and south-seeking poles of the compass needle as it rests on the paper. Use a ruler to connect and extend the north-south line established by the compass needle.

Remove the compass and, without moving the board, use the ruler to establish and draw a sight line to a distant object (see Figure 6). Be sure the sight line crosses the north-south line established by the compass. Repeat the process for a number of different objects. Then use a protractor, or the compass, to find the direction to each of the objects sighted. The direction can be measured in terms of degrees east or west of the north-south compass line.

Find the approximate magnetic declination for the location in which you are working (see Figure 1b). Use that information and the data you have collected to establish the direction of each of the objects sighted in terms of true north.

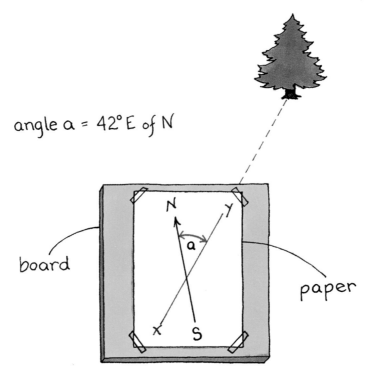

angle a = 42° E of N

Figure 6. The line N-S was established with a compass. Line X-Y is a sight line to a distant tree. It is found to be 42° east of the north established by the compass. What is the tree's direction relative to true north?

USING A COMPASS
TO DRAW A MAP

MATERIALS
- *materials used in Activity 7*
- *long stick*
- *playground or other large area*
- *measuring tape*

You can use the materials you used in Activity 7 to make a map of a playground, lawn, or field. Establish a north-south line on the paper using the compass as you did in Activity 7. Ask a friend to hold a stick upright at one corner or some other boundary marker of the area you are mapping. Then use your ruler to mark a sight line to the stick along the paper on the board. With a measuring tape, find the distance from the board to the marker you sighted. Repeat this procedure for the other corners or boundary markers of the area.

Use the data you collect to draw a map of the area (see Figure 7). You will need to establish a convenient scale for your map. The map shown in Figure 7 uses a scale of 1 cm = 10 m. That is, each centimeter on the map represents a distance of 10 m on the playground, lawn, or field. What scale should you use for your map?

Magnetism, Compasses, and Navigation

According to the results obtained from a variety of experiments, we are quite certain that the atoms of certain elements act like magnets. In soft iron, for example, the atoms are arranged in helter-skelter

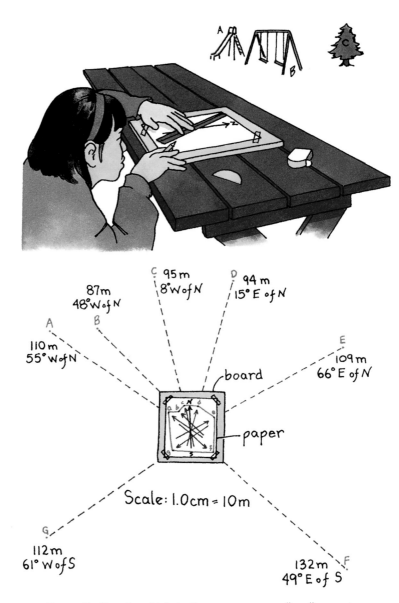

C 95 m
8° W of N

D 94 m
15° E of N

87m
48° W of N

A

B

110 m
55° W of N

E
109 m
66° E of N

board

paper

Scale: 1.0 cm = 10 m

G

112 m
61° W of S

132 m
49° E of S

F

Figure 7. The line N-S is the compass needle alignment. Points A, B, C, D, E, F, and G are points on the field being mapped. Distances to these points from the board and observer are given for each point along with angles from north and south. Points, a, b, c, d, e, f, and g are points on the map that correspond to points A, B, C, D, E, F, and G on the field.

fashion so that the magnetic effects of the atoms cancel one another as shown in Figure 8a. By stroking the iron with a magnet, the atoms align themselves with their magnetic poles all pointing in the same direction. Thus, the entire piece of iron acts like a magnet (see Figure 8b). If the iron is heated or dropped, the atoms lose their parallel magnetic alignment and the iron loses its magnetism.

Magnets made of steel or various alloys of nickel, aluminum, cobalt, and iron are called permanent magnets. Once magnetized, their atoms tend to remain aligned.

Compass needles made of permanent magnets will remain magnetized for long periods of time. These compasses are used exten-

a.

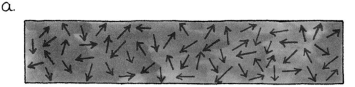

b.

N 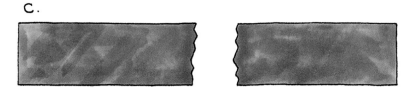 S

c.

Figure 8: a. A piece of iron in which the atomic magnets are in a state of disorder. The north-seeking ends of these tiny magnets, represented by arrowheads, point in all directions. b. A piece of iron that has been magnetized by stroking it with a strong magnet. Notice that all the north poles of the atomic magnets now point in the same direction. c. If the magnet in b were broken in half as shown, how many north and south poles would you have? To check your answer, place several flat ceramic magnets together in a row. Now "break" the magnet you have made in half. Test the polarities of the ends of the magnets with a compass.

sively in navigation. A navigator who knows his or her longitude, latitude, and the magnetic declination of the area can plot a course to a destination. By keeping fixed the direction that the ship or plane is traveling relative to the compass needle, the navigator can take the shortest path to the destination.

Early navigators used the North Star or the Southern Cross constellation to establish latitude, a clock to establish longitude, and a compass to indicate direction of travel. Once the magnetic declinations at various points around the globe had been established, navigators could locate their position and direction of travel quite well. Today electronic navigational systems using communication satellites provide very accurate values of latitude and longitude, but compasses are still used to establish direction of travel.

Magnets are common in today's technology. To see just how common they are, make a list of all the places where magnets or magnetic materials are used.

Animal Magnetism—An Example of Ongoing Science

Various investigations show that animals make use of magnetism. There is evidence that homing pigeons, migrating birds, whales, and other animals have built-in "compass needles" that guide them.

In some places, the earth's magnetic field is not uniform. Consequently, a compass needle is turned off its normal direction by a few degrees. This is usually the result of deposits of iron ore that create a small magnetic effect of their own. At Cornell University, Charles Walcott, who followed homing pigeons in his airplane, found that if pigeons are released in a nonuniform magnetic field region, they cannot orient themselves. Once outside the disturbed area, they immediately begin their homeward flight.

Walcott and William Keeton have attached tiny but powerful magnets to pigeons. On a clear day these birds have no difficulty finding home, but on cloudy days pigeons that would normally head for home seem to fly in random directions. This behavior suggests that the birds use the sun to orient themselves, and they use the earth's magnetism as a backup system of navigation. With strong magnets attached to their bodies, they can't detect the earth's weaker magnetism and so don't know which direction to follow to reach their roosts.

Careful examinations of pigeons have shown that there are small amounts of magnetic materials near muscles in their necks. How these tiny potential compasses might enable pigeons to find their way home is not well understood. But other scientists have found bits of magnetic materials in the skulls of dolphins, suggesting that they too have built-in compasses to guide them.

Joseph L. Kirschvink at the California Institute of Technology has studied the places where whales commonly become stranded. (Whales will sometimes swim onto beaches and become trapped there if the water is too shallow.) These stranding sites are at places where the earth's magnetism is weakest (magnetic lows). He believes that whales may follow magnetic lows in the oceans when they migrate and that they may blindly follow them onto beaches and become stranded.

Pilot whales may have become stranded by following the magnetic lows of the ocean.

Recently, magnetic crystals have been found within certain bacteria that live in water. Because bacteria consist of single cells, they are easy to study. The bacteria align their bodies in a north-south direction like a compass needle and move northward.

If the magnetism is reversed by placing a strong magnet near the bacteria, the animals move southward. When iron, which is found in the magnetic crystals inside the bacteria, is eliminated from the environment in which these bacteria live, they no longer orient themselves in any particular direction.

Some scientists believe that since compass needles in the Northern Hemisphere dip downward as well as point north, bacteria, by following their built-in compasses, are directed downward to the ocean sediment where they find food. This theory led to the idea that bacteria in a corresponding part of the Southern Hemisphere would swim southward (and downward)—the direction of sediment in that part of the world. When the same kind of bacteria were found near New Zealand, guess what? They do swim south! In fact, when some north-seeking bacteria were transferred to a place where south-seeking behavior was favored, they gradually died out and were replaced by south-swimming bacteria.

2

ELECTRIC CHARGE
AND ELECTRIC CELLS

Although electricity has been widely used for less than a century, it was discovered more than 2,500 years ago. It was again Thales, the Greek philosopher you met in Chapter 1, who found that when amber (a hard, yellowish substance) is rubbed with a cloth, it attracts other objects such as straw, feathers, and thread.

Others discovered that many substances, among them diamond, glass, sapphire, and rubber, attract light materials when rubbed with cloth. It was thought that rubbing creates an electric charge on the amber or other substances. Later, it was found that an electric charge cannot be created or destroyed. However, electric charges, which is what matter is made of, can be separated, and that is what happens when you rub amber, glass, plastic, rubber, and other substances. Metal cannot be charged in this manner because charges can move through metals into your body and from there to the earth. Metals are good conductors of electric charges. Amber, along with glass, rubber, and plastic are poor conductors. They are insulators. Charges tend to remain in place on these substances.

In your daily life, you see many common electrical effects that are caused by the separation of charges produced by rubbing materials together—static cling, sparks when you take off a wool sweater, a shock when you touch a doorknob after walking across a wool rug, and so on.

Two Kinds of Electric Charge

Experiments by Benjamin Franklin (1706–1790) and others showed that there are two kinds of electric charge—positive (+) and negative (-). You've seen that two north-seeking magnetic poles repel each other as do two south-seeking poles. Similarly, positive electric charges repel other positive charges and negative charges repel other negative charges. But positive charges attract negative charges just as a north-seeking magnetic pole attracts a south-seeking pole. Despite the similarities, magnets and charged objects have no effect on one another.

ACTIVITY 9

CHARGING THINGS

MATERIALS
- *balloons*
- *thread*
- *marking pen*
- *piece of cloth*
- *plastic sandwich bag*
- *clear plastic tape*
- *water faucet*
- *scissors*
- *steel wool*
- *sheet of paper*
- *plastic knitting needle*
- *wool cloth*

- *water*
- *clear plastic container*

(This activity will work best on a cold, clear, dry day. You may encounter difficulty if the weather is hot and humid because charges will leak away quickly in warm, damp air.) Inflate a balloon and suspend it from a thread as shown in Figure 9. Draw a circle on the balloon with a marking pen. Dry your hands thoroughly. Then rub the area inside the circle with a piece of cloth. If you have successfully separated charges, the balloon should have one charge and the cloth the opposite

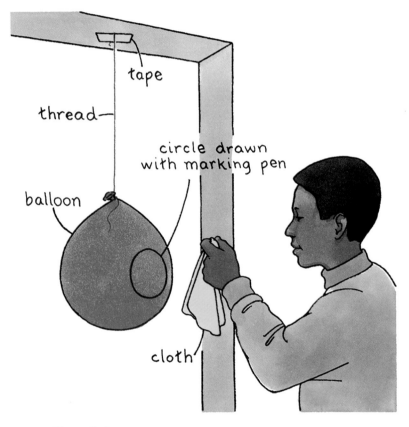

Figure 9. Because rubber is an insulator, a balloon can be charged in just one area—within the circle.

charge. If this is the case, what should happen when the cloth is brought slowly toward the circle on the balloon? Try it! Were you right?

Next, inflate a second balloon to about the same size as the first. Make a circle on the balloon and charge it in the same way as before. Bring the two charged circular areas near each other. Why do you think the circular area on the first balloon turns away when you bring the circle on a second balloon close to it?

Now inflate and suspend two more balloons, and draw a circle on each one. Charge the circle on one balloon by rubbing it with a plastic sandwich bag. Charge the circle on the second balloon by rubbing it with the part of your palm that is at the base of your thumb. What happens when you bring these two charged circles near one another? What does this tell you?

Charges can be separated in many ways. For example, cut off a piece of clear plastic tape about 20 cm (8 in.) long. Attach one end to the top of a door frame or kitchen cabinet. Cut off another similar piece and bring it near the first piece. What happens? Are the charges on the two pieces of tape the same or opposite?

Now take the two strips you cut from the roll. Fold over one end of each strip so that you have tabs that will not stick to your fingers. Place the sticky side of one strip on the non-sticky side of the other strip. Now grip the tab on each strip and pull the strips apart. What happens when you bring the strips near one another? Are the charges on the strips the same or opposite?

Rub another inflated balloon on your clothing and hold it against a wall. You'll find that the balloon sticks to the wall even though the wall has not been charged by rubbing. Charges in the wall, opposite in sign to those on the balloon, are attracted to the balloon, while like charges in the wall are repelled farther from the balloon (see Figure 10). Because the force between charges decreases with distance, the attractive forces of unlike charges is greater than the repulsion of like charges. We say that charges in the wall are induced to move by the charged balloon.

Rub another inflated balloon on your clothing and bring it near a thin stream of water flowing from a faucet. Does water respond to a charged object? Since water is not charged, how can you explain the attraction between water and the charged balloon?

Use scissors to cut a small wad of steel wool into *very* short lengths over a sheet of paper. Next, charge a plastic knitting needle by rubbing it vigorously with a woolen cloth. Are the pieces of metal attracted by the charged needle?

Place one of the tiny pieces of steel on the surface of some water in a clear plastic container. When the surface is calm, slowly bring the tip of a charged plastic knitting needle near the tiny piece of steel. Notice how the steel seems to be repelled by the needle. Can you explain why? Watch carefully as

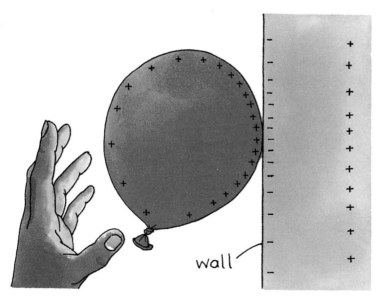

Figure 10. A charged balloon sticks to a wall because it attracts opposite charges and repels like charges in the wall.

you bring the tip of the charged needle near the water. What happens to the surface of the water as the needle gets very close to it?

Now dim or darken the room. Charge the knitting needle by rubbing it as hard and fast as you can with the cloth. With a very steady hand bring it close to the water. Watch for a tiny spark to jump from the needle to the hill of water. But wait! As charges from farther up the needle move down, another spark will jump to a newly formed hill of water. How many sparks can you get to jump from one charging of the needle?

Static Charge

The charges you produced by rubbing a balloon are called static charges because they do not move. They remain on the balloon or any other insulator. But experiments show that these static charges are the same as the charges that move inside batteries or wires connected to batteries.

Scientific studies of static electricity have provided inventors with the basis for technology that uses static charges. For example, static electricity is used in photocopiers to make copies of documents (see Figure 11). A positive charge is applied to a selenium plate. Then an image of the document is projected onto the plate in much the same way that an overhead projector makes an image on a screen. Selenium will conduct charge in the presence of light. As a result, a charge remains on only the dark parts of the image on the plate. A dark toner powder, which has been negatively charged, is then applied to the drum. The positive charges on the dark parts of the image attract the toner. When paper is applied to the plate, the powder is transferred from the drum to the paper. The paper now carries the dark parts of the image that were originally on the plate. The paper is heated to seal the toner powder to the paper, and a warm paper copy of the original image comes out of the photocopier.

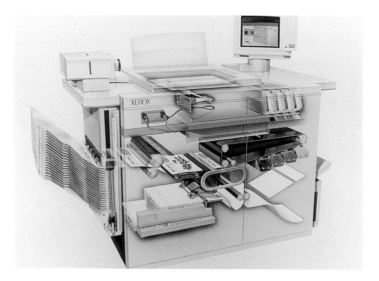

Diagram of a Xerox photocopier

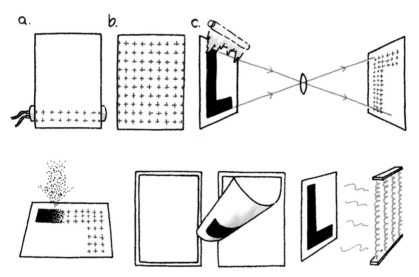

Figure 11: Static charge is used in the xerographic method of copying. In a and b a static charge is applied to a plate. c. The image to be copied is projected onto the plate. Charge is removed from those regions where light strikes the plate. d. Toner powder is applied. The powder sticks to the charges. e. Paper is pressed onto the plate, and the image is transferred to the paper. f. The image is fixed to the paper by heating.

Long before photocopiers, Benjamin Franklin invented lightning rods to protect buildings from damage. During a thunderstorm, a negative static charge builds up on the bottoms of clouds and a positive charge on their tops. Pointed lightning rods, which are made of metal, allow an exchange of positive and negative charges between earth and cloud as shown in Figure 12. This exchange reduces the charge on the cloud and the chances of a lightning strike. If a huge flow of charges does occur (a lightning stroke), it will move first along the path of the charge flow between lightning rod and cloud. When the charges reach the lightning rod, which is a very good conductor, they will flow along the rod to the earth without causing serious damage to the building.

Figure 12. A lightning rod provides a path to help discharge a cloud or to allow large amounts of charge in a lightning stroke to pass safely between cloud and ground.

Electric storms can cause multiple cloud-to-ground lightning strikes.

Static electric charges in electrostatic precipitators are used to remove particles from industrial smokestacks. Such precipitators can greatly reduce air pollution. Static electricity is used in a somewhat similar way to trap smoke, pollen, and other small particles in household air cleaners. Static charge induces charges on the polluting particles (see Figure 10). The particles are then attracted to the static charge on the precipitators just as charges in a wall are attracted to a charged balloon. Can you find other places where static charge is used in technology?

Oersted Provides a Connecting Link

For centuries, magnetism and electricity appeared to be unrelated. Rubbed amber had no effect on a magnet. Similarly, a magnet had no effect on static charges. But then, in 1819, Hans Christian Oersted (1777–1851) made a startling discovery—a discovery that eventually led to today's electrical technology. You can repeat what Oersted did and share in his discovery.

ACTIVITY 10

THE CONNECTION BETWEEN
ELECTRICITY AND MAGNETISM

MATERIALS
- *1-m (1-yd) length of insulated copper wire*
- *knife or wire stripper*
- *magnetic compass*
- *D-cell (flashlight battery)*

Obtain a meter-long piece of insulated wire. Have an adult help you remove about 3 cm (1 in.) of the insulation from each end of the wire. Place the center of the wire over a magnetic compass as shown in Figure 13. Be sure the wire is parallel to the compass needle. Now touch the bare ends of the wire to the opposite poles of a D-cell. **(Don't touch the wires to the battery for very long. The battery will wear out quickly under such conditions.)** What happens to the compass needle when you do this?

When the wire is connected to the D-cell, electric charge flows along the wire from one pole of the battery to the other. This flow of charge is called an electric current.

Do the experiment again with the wire under the compass. What is different this time? What happens if you turn the battery around and repeat the experiment?

The effect you have seen is due to the magnetic field that

Figure 13. What happens to the compass needle when charge flows in the wire?

surrounds a moving charge. Oersted made this discovery by accident. But his discovery illustrates what scientist Louis Pasteur (1822–1895) said decades later, "Accident favors the prepared mind." Oersted was very interested in the similarities between electricity and magnetism and thought the two must be related in some way. It is likely that others had seen the same effect but paid no attention. Because Oersted believed that electricity and magnetism were related and because he had studied them carefully, he was prepared to notice an effect that he stumbled upon.

To avoid becoming lost, you might carry a compass on a hike through the country. In a city, a map of the streets would probably be more useful, but just for fun, take the compass with you on a subway ride. Watch the compass as you move from station to station. Can you explain the behavior of your compass?

A CURRENT DETECTOR

MATERIALS
- *small magnetic compass*
- *clay*
- *5 m (5.5 yd) of #22, #24, or #26 enamel-coated copper wire*
- *sandpaper*
- *D-cell (flashlight battery)*
- *masking tape*

Shortly after Oersted's discovery, André Ampère (1775–1836) used Oersted's discovery to invent the galvanoscope, a device that detects electric current. You can make a simple galvanoscope for yourself. All you need is a magnetic compass and a long piece of enamel-coated copper wire. The enamel forms an insulating layer around the wire.

Cut a piece of the wire about 5 m (5.5 yd) long and wind it into a coil by wrapping it around the compass. Be sure to wind all the wire in the same direction. Leave about 30 cm (12 in.) of uncoiled wire at each end. A piece of masking tape wound around each side of the coil will keep the wires in place. Remove the coil from the compass and use sandpaper to remove about 2 cm (1 in.) of the insulation from each of the two uncoiled ends of the wire.

To see that your galvanoscope does detect electric current, use a little clay to hold the coil and compass in place as shown in Figure 14. Be sure the wires in the coil are parallel with the compass needle. Tap the compass gently to free the needle.

What happens to the compass needle when you connect the bare ends of the two leads from the coil to opposite poles of a D-cell? **(Don't connect the coil to the D-cell for long or you'll wear out the cell.)**

Volta and Electric Cells

By 1750, scientists knew that electricity, unlike gravity, could cause either attraction or repulsion. (Gravity is always an attraction force.) They also knew that while an electric charge would stay at rest on insulators, it could also move along conductors. But they had not

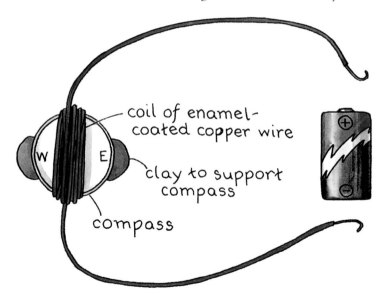

Figure 14. A galvanoscope can be made from a magnetic compass and a coil of wire.

found a way to maintain a steady flow of charge. Once a spark carried a charge from an insulator to the earth, the charge was gone in a flash.

The Italian biologist Luigi Galvani (1737–1798), while dissecting frogs, noticed that a frog's leg would twitch whenever it was touched by two different metals. Until his death, Galvani believed that the electricity came from the muscle tissue. He called it *animal electricity*.

Alessandro Volta (1745–1827) questioned Galvani's notion that the twitching of a frog's muscle arose from electricity generated within the animal. To prove his point, Volta tried to produce electric effects without any animal tissue. He knew that two different metals were needed to make a frog's muscle twitch and that salty water was a good conductor. He put these two facts together to construct the world's first battery. Volta placed strips of copper and zinc in bowls of salt solution similar to the arrangement seen in Figure 15a. With about 30 of these cups arranged in series (one after the other), a person touching the copper at one end and the zinc at the other would get a shock. But it was not a short shock like the kind you receive when you touch a metal doorknob after walking across a wool rug. It was a continuous shock. If the wires from the two ends (electrodes) of such a battery were brought close together, a spark would "jump." But, again, the spark, like the shock, was continuous. One spark did not remove all the electric energy stored in the battery. Volta had succeeded in developing a device that would cause charges to move continuously.

In 1800, he built what came to be known as a "voltaic pile." It was a more compact and drier version of his original battery. He made a pile by stacking a piece of copper, a felt disc soaked in salt water, and a piece of zinc. Then he repeated the trio again and again (see Figure 15b). When he connected the final piece of copper at the top to the zinc at the bottom, electric charges flowed continuously from one side of the battery to the other.

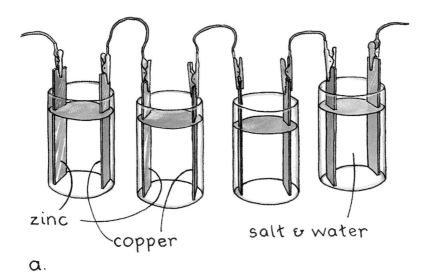

zinc

copper

salt & water

a.

copper

zinc

felt soaked in salt water

b.

Figure 15: a. A modern example of Volta's first battery. b. A diagram of a voltaic pile.

Volta found that if he held strips of zinc and copper together at one end, he could feel a "tingle" when he placed his tongue between the other ends of the strips. Place the edges of a clean penny and a clean quarter against your tongue. Then touch the coins together. You may be able to feel a slight tingle caused by the flow of charge. When the coins act as an electric cell, one metal dissolves as it releases a charge. Can you sense a metallic taste when you remove the coins?

★ ACTIVITY 12

MAKING BATTERIES

MATERIALS
- *paper towels*
- *2 tablespoons salt dissolved in 1 glass of water*
- *shiny penny and dime*
- *galvanoscope*
- *sandpaper*
- *zinc sheet about 10 cm (4 in.) square*
- *ammonium chloride (borrow some from your science teacher)*
- *copper sheet or screen about 8 cm (3 in.) square*
- *insulated wires, bare ends*
- *1.5-volt flashlight bulb such as GE #48*

To see how Volta made his battery, you can build one electric cell and test it with your galvanoscope. (A battery consists of two or more electric cells connected together.) Dip about 1/8 of a paper towel in a mixture of salt and water that you have stirred thoroughly. Fold the wet piece of towel so it is about the same size as a penny. Then place the wet towel between two shiny coins—a penny and a dime. Touch the bare end of one of the leads from your galvanoscope to the penny. Touch the bare end of the other lead to the dime. Watch the compass needle when the metals are connected to the galvanoscope. What happens? What does it tell you?

Make a battery by stacking two cells together—a small voltaic pile. To make a more powerful cell, use sandpaper to clean the sheet of zinc. Put the zinc on some newspapers. Fold a paper towel so it is several layers thick and a little larger than the zinc sheet. Soak the towel in a solution that contains as much ammonium chloride as you can dissolve in half a glass of water. Place the wet towel on the zinc sheet. Then put a sheet of copper that you have sanded clean or copper screening (about the same size as the zinc sheet) on top of the wet towel as shown in Figure 16.

Figure 16. A copper-zinc cell can be used to light a flashlight bulb. A bulb holder can be made from a plastic film canister, aluminum foil, and a coin. Holes in the top and side of the canister will support the bulb and lower wire. The top wire can be held firmly against the side of the bulb by the hole in the canister cap. The coin ensures good contact between the base of the bulb and the aluminum foil.

Use your battery to light a small 1.5-volt flashlight bulb. (A GE #48 flashlight bulb in a small bulb holder works well.) Connect the zinc sheet to one side of the bulb holder with an insulated wire. Connect the copper sheet to the other side of the bulb holder with a second wire. (If you don't have a bulb holder, you can make one from a plastic 35-mm film canister, a coin, and aluminum foil as shown in Figure 16.) Be sure that the wires make good contact with the metal sheets. Push down on the copper sheet or screen so as to squeeze together the three layers of your battery. You should be able to see the bulb's filament glow. It can be seen best in a dark or dimly lighted room. If you have trouble, try wetting the towel in the ammonium chloride solution again.

Battery Technology

Volta showed the world that a constant flow of electric charge could be produced by using two different metals and an electrolyte (a wet or moist material or a solution that will conduct electricity). Since Volta's discovery, battery technology has made giant strides. In dry cells, such as the flashlight cell shown in Figure 17, Volta's wet electrolyte has been replaced with a black paste made of powdered carbon, manganese dioxide, and a solution of ammonium chloride. The positive electrode is a carbon rod, which is immersed in the electrolyte paste. A zinc can serves as the negative electrode. It is covered with an insulating layer of cardboard that is often sealed inside a steel container. The inside surface of the zinc is coated with a porous material that separates the metal from the paste. The pores allow the passage of the ammonium chloride solution but keep the carbon and manganese dioxide from touching the zinc.

When the electrodes are connected with a conductor, such as wires and a bulb, chemical reactions taking place inside the cell

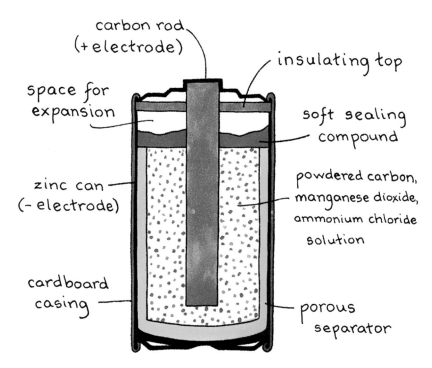

carbon rod
(+ electrode)

insulating top

space for
expansion

soft sealing
compound

zinc can
(- electrode)

powdered carbon,
manganese dioxide,
ammonium chloride
solution

cardboard
casing

porous
separator

Figure 17. Dry cells like this one are used in flashlights and many other battery-operated devices.

cause negative charges (electrons) to flow through the conductor from the zinc to the carbon. Inside the cell there is a flow of charged atoms (ions). Positive ions flow toward the carbon, and negative ions flow toward the zinc.

Smaller electric cells, often called button batteries, can be found in various electrical devices ranging from watches to the pacemakers used to control human heartbeats. Many of these cells use powdered zinc as the negative electrode, mercury oxide as the positive electrode, and an alkaline electrolyte. They will provide small electric currents for a long time, making these cells very useful in devices such as pacemakers, where the batteries cannot be changed easily.

Dry cells are very useful, but they cannot be used a second time. Once they are worn out, they must be replaced. Such cells are called primary cells. Secondary cells, on the other hand, can be recharged and used over and over again. The most common secondary cell is the lead storage cell. Three, six, or twelve such cells can be connected one after the other to make 6-volt, 12-volt, or 24-volt batteries, which are found in cars, golf carts, and other places where large electric currents are required and household electricity is not available or convenient to use.

In a lead storage cell, lead is the negative electrode and lead oxide is the positive electrode. Because sulfuric acid is used as the electrolyte, these batteries are enclosed in a nonmetallic material such as hard rubber. Lead storage cells are connected together to make a battery as shown in Figure 18. When the battery is used (discharges) to start a car, for example, the electrodes slowly change

A cutaway view of a lead storage battery

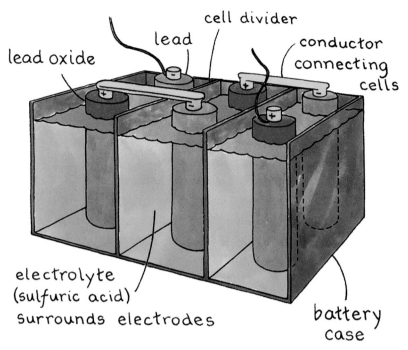

lead oxide

lead

cell divider

conductor
connecting
cells

electrolyte
(sulfuric acid)
surrounds electrodes

battery
case

Figure 18. A diagram of a 6-volt lead storage battery. It consists of three lead cells.

to lead sulfate. But the flow of current can be reversed and the battery recharged as the original electrode materials are reformed from lead sulfate. All cars are equipped with a generator that recharges the battery once the car starts. However, if someone leaves the headlights on for a long time while the engine is not running, the battery will continue to discharge. After a while, the battery will not be able to produce enough current to turn the starter.

In addition to these common cells or batteries, a great variety of other cells have been produced. All of them consist of electrodes made from two different materials and an electrolyte. They include the nickel-iron battery developed by Thomas Edison for heavy service use in such things as electric trucks; the nickel-cadmium battery, which is used in portable battery-operated equipment such as electric shavers, radios, and television sets; silver-zinc batteries that can develop large currents for short periods of time; and silver-cadmium batteries, which can be used in place of silver-zinc batteries where longer discharge times are needed.

In many cases, such as the development of the nickel-iron battery, the technology was developed without a thorough understanding of the science (chemistry) that drives the electric charge. Edison, who was known for his trial-and-error approach, developed a battery that worked. He was not interested in studying the chemistry needed to explain how it worked.

Today, battery research continues. Scientists at Arizona State University have developed a new kind of electrolyte—a rubbery substance made by dissolving polymers in lithium salts. (Polymers are large molecules made by linking together many small identical molecules.) Many researchers believe that this new electrolyte will degenerate less rapidly. Such a lightweight, rechargeable battery would be widely used in laptop computers and cellular telephones.

Batteries and Electroplating

By the middle of the nineteenth century, silversmiths had learned how to use batteries to cover the base metal of a candlestick, for example, with a thin layer of silver or gold. The base metal was usually german silver, a mixture of copper, nickel, and zinc. The base metal was immersed in a solution containing a salt of silver or gold and was connected to the negative electrode of a battery. The positive electrode of the battery was sometimes connected to a chunk of silver or gold immersed in the same solution. As, say, positively charged silver ions from the solution plated onto the base metal, silver ions from the chunk connected to the positive pole of the battery dissolved in the solution, replacing those that had plated out.

PLATING COPPER

MATERIALS

- *copper sulfate (See your science teacher or a store that supplies materials for swimming pools.) Keep away from mouth and eyes.*
- *glass*
- *water*
- *6-volt dry cell battery*
- *old metal spoons or carbon rods*
- *insulated wires*
- *spring-type clothespins or alligator clips on ends of wires*

To see how a metal is plated, ask an adult to help you dissolve one or two teaspoonfuls of blue copper sulfate crystals in a glass of warm water. Then use insulated wires to connect the poles of a 6-volt dry cell battery to two old spoons or carbon rods immersed in the blue solution of copper sulfate (see Figure 19). Clothespins will help fasten the bare ends of the wires to the electrodes and hold them in place if you don't have wires with alligator clips.

    Watch the spoons or rods as the plating proceeds. Does copper collect on the spoon or rod that is connected to the positive (+) or to the negative (-) pole of the battery? What does this result suggest about the charge on the copper ions in solution? Does the amount of copper deposited depend on how long the battery is connected?

insulated
wires

6-volt
dry cell
battery

spoons or carbon rods

copper sulfate
in water

Figure 19. A battery and a solution of copper sulfate can be used to plate copper on old spoons or carbon rods.

3

THE UNION OF ELECTRICITY
AND MAGNETISM

Oersted's discovery that there was a magnetic field around a moving charge led almost immediately to new technology. William Sturgeon (1783–1850) found, probably by accident, that if the wires of a coil were wrapped around an iron core, the strength of the magnetic field was concentrated in the iron. By varnishing a U-shaped piece of iron to insulate it from the metal wire, Sturgeon was able to lift a 4-kg (9-lb) weight with a 0.2-kg (7-oz) iron core.

Using wire insulated by silk strips torn from his wife's old dresses, Joseph Henry (1797–1878) was able to wrap layer after layer of wire around an iron core. In a demonstration at Yale University in 1831, Henry lifted more than a ton of iron with his electromagnet.

Today, as you can see in the photograph, this technology is used to lift and move huge piles of scrap metal.

AN ELECTROMAGNET

MATERIALS
- *about 1 m (1 yd) of #22, #24, or #26 enamel-coated wire*
- *iron nail*
- *sandpaper*
- *D-cell (flashlight battery)*
- *paper clips*

You can make a small electromagnet by wrapping about a meter (yd) of enameled copper wire around an iron nail. Be sure to always wrap the wire in the same direction. Use sandpaper to remove the enamel from the ends of the wire and connect them to a D-cell. How many paper clips can your electromagnet lift? **(Don't connect the electromagnet to the battery for very long. The battery will wear out quickly under such conditions.)**

How many paper clips can you lift with the coil if you take out the nail?

Rewind the wire around the nail again, but this time wind half the turns in one direction and the other half in the opposite direction. Predict the number of paper clips your electromagnet will lift now. Were you right?

An electromagnet is used to lift and move aluminum cans at a recycling depot.

FARADAY AND ELECTRIC MOTORS

MATERIALS
- *four to six ceramic disk or rectangular magnets*
- *tape*
- *long (about 80 cm or 30 in.) flexible insulated wire*
- *knife or wire strippers*
- *6-volt dry cell battery*
- *Styrofoam cup*
- *two large paper clips*
- *sandpaper*
- *30 cm (1 ft) of enameled copper wire*
- *two wires with alligator clips*

Michael Faraday (1791–1867) made the world's first electric motor. It was more a toy than a practical machine. But it was based on the interaction between electric currents and magnets—a new science developed by Faraday, Oersted, Ampère, and others. The basic principle underlying Faraday's and all other electric motors can be demonstrated quite easily.

Place four or six ceramic magnets so that they attract and form a column. Separate the column magnet at its middle. Leave a gap of about 1 cm (⅜ in.) between the faces of the two magnets. Use tape to keep the magnets in place at this separation. Place a loop, made from the center of a long, flexible insulated wire, between the faces of the magnets as shown in Figure 20. The ends of the wire should be bare. If they are not, ask an adult to remove the insulation from the last 2 cm (1 in.) of each end. Tape the wire in place as shown. Then touch the bare ends of the wire to the opposite poles of a D-cell. Notice that the loop of wire between the faces of the magnets is pushed either up or down. Which

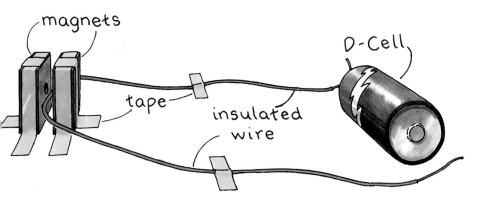

Figure 20. The basic principles of the electric motor can be seen by using the materials shown in this diagram.

way is it pushed? What happens to the direction in which the wire is pushed if you turn the D-cell around? How do you think this basic principle is used in building an electric motor?

You can apply this principle in building a very simple little electric motor. To begin, make a stand for your motor. Invert a Styrofoam cup. Then unfold one end of each of the two large paper clips. Tape them to opposite sides of the cup as shown in Figure 21. Place two disk or rectangular ceramic magnets on the top of the inverted cup. Place a third magnet inside the cup and directly beneath the other two. This procedure will add strength to the magnet and help to hold it in place.

The coil, which forms the turning part of the motor, can be made by winding about 30 cm (1 ft) of enameled copper wire three or four times around your first two fingers. Leave some extra wire on each end. Wrap these ends around opposite sides of the coil several times to help keep the coil wires in place. Two tiny pieces of tape can be used to hold the wires of the coil in place as shown in Figure 21. The unwrapped end pieces should be about 5 cm (2 in.) long. Straighten and then sandpaper these ends to remove the enamel. The sandpapered ends of the coil fit into the loops you made with the paper clips (see Figure 21). Turn the coil gently. It should come very close to the top of the magnet. If necessary, adjust the position of the paper-clip supports.

Use wires with alligator clips on each end to connect the poles of a 6-volt dry cell to the paper clips that support the coil of the motor. Give the coil a gentle flip and watch it spin.

Actually, this motor should not work. Motors that are operated by a battery (DC motors) have a commutator—a device that stops the current in the coil every half turn. Without the commutator, such motors would make only half a turn. Then the force of the magnetic field on the current that you

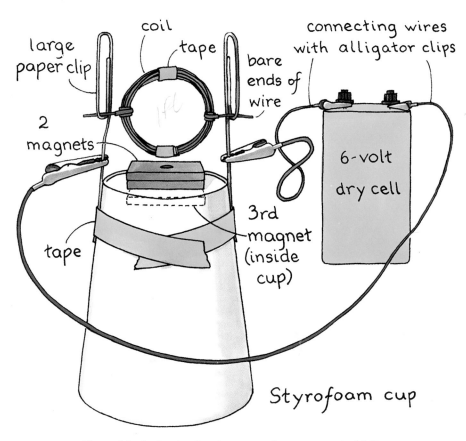

Figure 21. A simple electric motor that you can build illustrates the use of the basic principle discovered by Faraday.

saw earlier in this activity would simply stretch the coil; the coil would not turn any longer.

In the simple motor you made, the coil is so light that it bounces on the paper-clip loops and breaks the electrical connection, allowing the coil to rotate past the point where it would simply be stretched.

Today electric motors of various designs are everywhere. To understand how important Faraday's discovery was, make a list of all the devices you can think of that use electric motors.

Faraday and Electricity From Magnets

Faraday, like many other scientists, held a firm belief in the symmetry of nature. Since electric current produces a magnetic field, Faraday reasoned that it should be possible to produce an electric current from magnetic fields. To test his reasoning, Faraday made very strong magnets and placed them near wire coils. Nothing happened. He used bigger magnets and more coils of wire; still nothing. Then, on Christmas day in 1831, Faraday found the effect he was looking for. He had connected a battery to a coil of wire wrapped around one side of an iron ring. On the other side of the ring, as shown in Figure 22, he had wrapped a separate coil of wire. When he closed the switch between the battery and the coil, the galvanoscope indicated a current. When he opened the switch, the needle moved again, but in the opposite direction.

When he saw the galvanoscope move, Faraday realized that the key to producing an electric current with magnets was to change the magnetic field. A steady field has no effect. Oersted had shown that an electric charge has to be moving to produce a magnetic field. Now Faraday discovered that a magnetic field had to be changing to make charges move.

Faraday pictured a magnetic field as lines like those in the pattern made by the iron filings in Activity 1. Whenever the number of field lines through a coil of wire increased or decreased, a charge was forced to move in the wires. Or, if a wire moved across magnetic field lines, a force was exerted on charges in the wire.

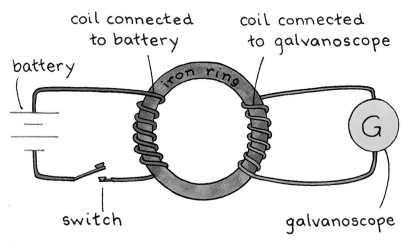

Figure 22. The experimental apparatus used by Faraday to produce an electric current from a changing magnetic field. The standard symbol for an electric cell is shown. In the diagram, two cells are connected to form a battery.

★ **ACTIVITY 16**

BUILD AN ELECTRIC
GENERATOR

MATERIALS

- *galvanoscope*
- *coil of wire—make from about 5 m (5.5 yd) of #22, #24, or #26 enamel-coated wire*
- *strong magnet*
- *wires to connect coil and galvanoscope*

Figure 23 is a diagram of a simple electric generator—a generator that Faraday often used in his lectures and one that you can build by following the diagram.

Be sure the galvanoscope is far enough away so that the magnet has no effect on it. Notice that as you move the magnet in and out of the coil, an electric current is detected by the galvanoscope.

Which way does the compass needle turn when the south-seeking pole of the magnet is pushed into the coil? When the north-seeking pole is pushed into the coil? Which way does it turn when the magnet is pulled out of the coil? Does the speed with which you move the magnet affect the current induced? Is there any effect if you don't move the magnet? Can you produce a current by moving the coil instead of the magnet? What happens if you use half as many turns of wire in the coil?

Figure 23. A simple electric generator similar to one used by Faraday.

As you have seen, electric current flows one way when the magnet is pushed into the coil and the other way when it is pulled out. This to-and-fro movement of the charges is called an alternating current (AC). Electric currents produced by batteries move in one direction. Such a movement of an electric charge is called direct current (DC). The needle in your galvanoscope was deflected one way or the other when connected to a battery. It did not swing back and forth.

To obtain a direct current, like the one you get from a battery, Faraday built a generator like the one in Figure 24. When he rotated the copper disk, charges within the metal were constantly being moved in the same direction across magnetic field lines. As a result, the charges were always pushed in the same di-

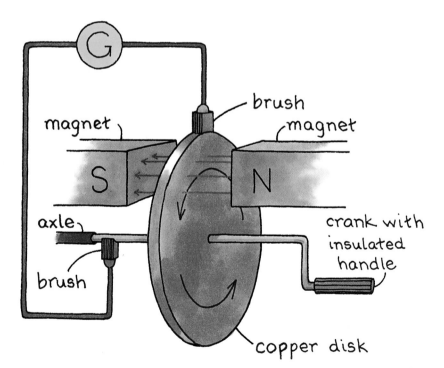

Figure 24. Faraday's DC generator is shown in this diagram.

rection. A metal brush (see Figure 24) resting on the axle allowed the charge to flow through the galvanometer and back to the edge of the disk. There, another brush made contact with the copper.

Men working inside a large electric power generator

Today's electric generators and motors are much larger and more complicated than Faraday's, but they are based on the same principles. Figure 25 is a diagram of a very simple generator. The coil, which may consist of thousands of turns of wire, rotates in a magnetic field. As the coil turns, the number of field lines through the coil is constantly changing, causing the charges in the wires to move. The motion of the charge constitutes an electric current. Wires connected by brushes make contact with the coil through rings, and a charge can be conducted by the wires to places far from the generator.

Figure 25 shows an AC generator. A DC generator can be built by adding a commutator. The commutator changes the connections to the coil every half turn so that current always flows in one direction.

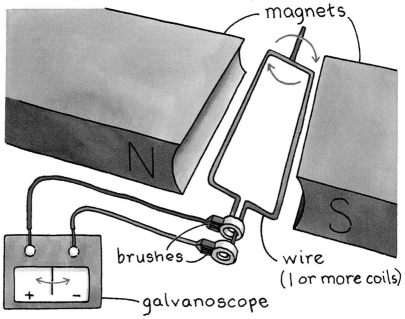

Figure 25. A simple AC generator is shown here. When the coil is turned in the magnetic field, an electric current is generated in the wire. The galvanoscope shows that the current is reversed every half turn of the coil. Therefore, the current is an alternating current.

The electrical energy in your home or school is produced by giant AC generators in power stations. The photograph shows the coils in one such generator. A rotator containing the magnet fits in the opening that extends through the center of the coils. In most commercial generators, it is the magnet that rotates, thus eliminating the need for brushes, which wear out quickly. The generator shown in the photograph is 18 m (59 ft) long, 4 m (13 ft) in diameter, and weighs nearly 800 tons.

The rotors of such huge generators are turned by steam or water turbines. Steam is generated by burning fossil fuel (coal, oil, or natural gas) or is produced in a nuclear reactor. Water turbines are powered by moving water falling over a dam or flowing along a river.

4

THE LIGHTING
OF AMERICA

Faraday discovered the secret of generating a steady flow of charge in 1831, but electric lights were not common in homes until the twentieth century. It was not practical to use steam or flowing water to produce electricity for factories. The factories could save a step, and lots of money, by using steam engines or water wheels to turn the belts and gears required to get work done.

When an electric current passes through a thin wire, the wire becomes hot. In 1879, Thomas Edison (1847–1931) used this principle to make a practical electric light. He used a thin wire filament inside a clear glass bulb from which he removed the air. The filament became so hot that it glowed brightly.

Humphry Davy (1778–1829) had invented the carbon arc lamp around 1820. Such lamps were used in factories along the Niagara River, where electrical energy was first generated in significant amounts in the 1880s. But these lights were too bright, noisy, and unsteady for household use. Gas lights were much more practical.

The intensity of the light from Edison's bulbs could be controlled by the size and nature of the filament inside. The safety and ease of control of the light—the flip of a switch was all it took—led more and more people to use electricity to light their homes.

Generating Electricity

The first electric generating station for incandescent lights was opened in New York City in 1882 under Edison's direction. Edison's power plant generated direct current. However, George Westinghouse (1846–1914), founder of the company that bears his name and inventor of the air brake, proposed that AC be used to transmit electric energy.

Westinghouse and Edison knew that it would be difficult to transmit DC electric energy over great distances. Much of the energy would be converted to heat. Therefore, Edison proposed that electric power plants be numerous and close to the users. Westinghouse argued that with alternating current, transformers could be used to raise the voltage (energy per charge) to thousands of volts. At such high voltages, the electric current could be small, and the electric energy converted to heat in wires would be greatly reduced. Other transformers could reduce voltages to reasonable levels before the energy entered homes, schools, or factories. In this way, electric energy could be transmitted over large distances so that rural dwellers and farmers, as well as cities, could be supplied with electricity.

The transformer, together with Nikola Tesla's invention of the AC motor, which was vastly superior to the DC motor, enabled Westinghouse to win the battle. The electrification of America, which was not completed until World War II, was done with AC, not DC. Figure 26 shows how electric energy is transmitted from a power plant to individual homes or factories.

Electricity and the Future

Most electric energy today is produced by burning fossil fuels. This practice poses two problems for the future of electricity. First, the supply of fossil fuels is limited. Eventually, we will run out of oil, coal, and natural gas. Second, when these fuels burn, one of the by-products is carbon dioxide because all fossil fuels contain carbon. For every gram of carbon that burns, 3.7 g of carbon dioxide are produced.

During the past century, the concentration of carbon dioxide in the atmosphere has increased by nearly 20 percent. Because carbon dioxide traps heat in much the same way that a greenhouse does, its increased concentration has given rise to what many call the greenhouse effect. It is an effect that many scientists believe is causing the earth's average temperature to rise—an effect that could cause

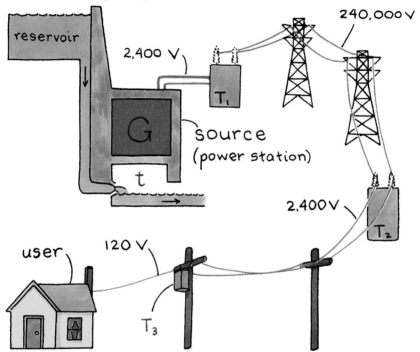

Figure 26. Transformers enable electric energy to be transmitted on high-voltage lines. Before the electricity enters a home, the voltage is reduced by another transformer. In this hydroelectric power station, moving water turns the turbine, t, which in turn powers the generator, G. A step-up transformer, T^1, raises the voltage from 2,400 volts to 240,000 volts for transmission. At a substation, a step-down transformer, T^2, lowers the voltage to 2,400 volts. Another stepdown transformer, T^3, on a line near the user, lowers the voltage to 120 or 240 volts before it enters the home.

dramatic changes in the climates. One thing is certain, we have to find substitutes for fossil fuels.

In an effort to reduce the use of fossil fuels, scientists are focusing on other ways of producing electricity. In California, for example, acres and acres of the ground are covered by wind turbines, whose spinning blades can be used to generate electricity.

In other places, mirrors focus sunlight on a boiler where the steam generated is used to produce electricity. Steam from deep within the earth is also used to turn turbines. This source of energy, known as geothermal energy, is presently limited to natural sites where the steam can be tapped. But scientists are looking for other places where this natural source of heat might provide a way to produce electric energy.

In some coastal areas, the movement of water in the daily tides turns turbines that power electric generators. Deep ocean water is generally colder than water at the surface, and this temperature difference can be harnessed to produce energy as well.

About 16 percent of the world's electricity is already generated in nuclear power plants. Many people, however, are concerned about the safety of such plants. They fear that nuclear accidents could release radioactive materials into the environment. While such concerns must be considered, it is also true that electricity generated in nuclear power plants releases no carbon dioxide into the atmosphere.

In the more distant future, vast arrays of photovoltaic cells in orbit about the earth may be used to generate microwave beams that will power electric generators around our globe.

Wind turbines provide power to a generating plant in California.

USING LIGHT
TO GENERATE ELECTRICITY

MATERIALS
- *insulated wires with alligator clips*
- *photovoltaic cells*
- *milliameter*
- *sun or lamp*

Small photovoltaic cells are becoming increasingly popular. Perhaps you have a pocket calculator or another device that obtains its electric energy from light. Your school may have a photovoltaic cell you can borrow, or you may buy one at a hobby shop or scientific supply house.

73

Use wires with alligator clips to connect the leads of a photovoltaic cell to a milliameter. Turn the dark side of the photovoltaic cell toward the sun or a lamp. What happens to the meter? What evidence do you have that light can be converted to electric energy? What happens if you cover the cell with your hand or place it in a shady place? What happens as you slowly change the angle between the light and the cell?

Electric Cars and the Future

Electric cars are not new, but they have never been able to compete with gasoline-powered cars. However, as concern over the increasing amounts of carbon dioxide in the atmosphere continues to grow, electric cars may be very common a decade from now. These cars, which release no carbon dioxide and are very quiet, will probably operate on batteries. Should their batteries be charged by using electricity generated by burning fossil fuels? If not, how else might the batteries be charged?

Electric vans, such as this ETX-II, may be a common form of transportation in the near future.

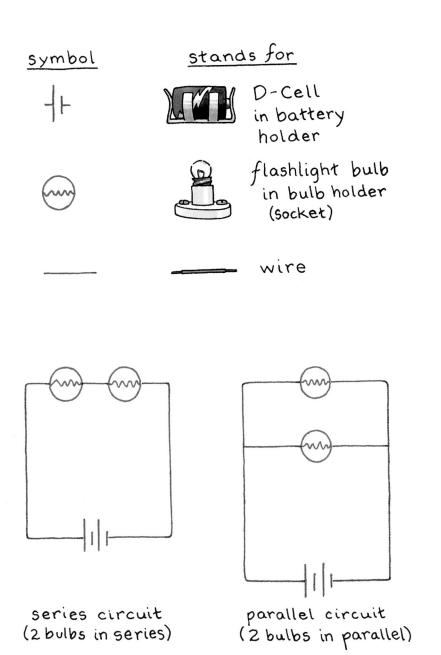

symbol	stands for
⊣⊢	D-Cell in battery holder
◯⎰⎱	flashlight bulb in bulb holder (socket)
———	wire

series circuit
(2 bulbs in series)

parallel circuit
(2 bulbs in parallel)

Figure 27: Schematic diagrams of a series circuit and a parallel circuit.

GOING FURTHER

In this book, the focus has been on the science and technology involved in generating electric energy. You have seen only a small portion of the way that electricity and magnetism are used in our culture. But even the limited topics developed here could fill several more books. A few of the things you might like to investigate are listed below.

★ • Use a clear plastic bottle, a cylindrical magnet sealed in a plastic tube, and iron filings to examine magnetic fields around a magnet in three dimensions.
★ • Obtain a piece of lodestone and investigate its properties.
★ • Design an experiment to measure the strength of a magnet.
• How did early navigators use clocks, compasses, and magnetic declinations to establish their latitude and longitude?
★ • How is static electricity used in an antistatic spray?
★ • As you've seen, objects that are insulators can be charged by rubbing them with cloth, plastic, fur, and so on. Can they be charged by rubbing them with paper?
★ • How can you tell whether the excess charge on a charged object is positive or negative?
★ • Under adult supervision, design an experiment to find out

which materials, among both solids and liquids, are good conductors of electricity and which are not.

★ • Use D-cells, bulbs, wire, and other materials to build your own flashlight.

★ • Use D-cells, wires, bulbs, and paper fasteners to build a quiz board. Users could choose alternate answers by touching a paper fastener beside the answer with a wire lead. A light goes on when a correct answer is chosen.

★ • Build a simple AC and DC electric generator. What is different about the generators? What is the same?

★ • How does a transformer work?

★ • Figure 27 shows two simple circuits that you can build using batteries, bulbs, and wires. One is a series circuit; the other a parallel circuit. Build both circuits and experiment with them by removing a bulb, comparing bulb brightness, and so on. After doing your experiments, do you think household circuits are wired in parallel or in series? Why?

★ • Design and build a model of an electric car.

★ • Design and build a model of a solar-powered car.

GLOSSARY

ampere (A): a unit that measures electric current in terms of charge flow per second.

alternating current (AC): a flow of electric charge that moves back and forth, flowing first in one direction and then in the opposite.

battery: two or more electrochemical cells connected in series—the negative pole of one connected to the positive pole of the next.

conductors: materials along which electric charges readily move.

direct current (DC): a flow of electric charge that moves in only one direction.

electric charge: the protons (positive charge) and electrons (negative charge) that make up matter. Like charges repel; unlike charges attract.

electric circuit: a battery and the electrical devices to which it is connected, such as bulbs, wires, motors, etc.

electric current: the flow of electric charge, which is measured in amperes.

electric generator: a device used to produce electricity by changing the magnetic field through a coil of wire.

electrochemical cell (electric cell): a devise containing an electrolyte (chemicals) and electrodes that serves as a source of electrical energy. Electric charges will flow from one pole of the cell to the other through circuit elements, such as wires, bulbs, motors, etc., that lie between the poles.

electromagnet: wire wound around an iron core that behaves like a magnet when an electric current flows through the wire.

electrons: negatively charged particles with very little mass. In atoms, the electrons make up the outer part of the atom that surrounds the nucleus.

electroplating: using electric current to plate metals from a solution of metallic salt. The electrode on which the metal is plated (deposited) is immersed in the solution and connected to the negative pole of an electric cell or power source. Another electrode also immersed in the solution is connected to the positive pole of the same electric cell.

galvanoscope: a devise consisting of a coil of wire wrapped around magnetic compass that is used to detect electric current.

insulators: poor conductors of electric charge.

magnetic compass: a magnetic needle mounted in a transparent container. In the earth's magnetic field, the needle orients itself in a north-south direction.

magnetic declination: the difference in angle between the compass reading and true north.

magnetic field: gives the direction and strength of the magnetic force around the poles of a magnet. The direction of the field is the direction the north-seeking pole of a compass needle points. The strength of a field is given by the concentration of the lines.

magnetic poles: a magnet has two poles—north and south. The north pole is the end of the magnet that points in a northerly direction if the magnet is free to turn. Magnetic field lines, by definition, run from south pole to north pole. Opposite magnetic poles attract; like magnetic poles repel.

nucleus: the tiny central core of an atom, which contains positively charged protons along with neutrons, which carry no charge but have the same mass as the protons.

protons: the positively charged particles of matter. They are found in the nuclei of atoms.

static charges: charges that do not move but remain wherever they are, which is usually on insulators.

transformer: a devise used to raise or lower the voltage (energy per charge) in an electric circuit.

volt (V): a unit that measures electric energy per charge.

UNITS AND THEIR ABBREVIATIONS

LENGTH

English	Metric
mile (mi)	kilometer (km)
yard (yd)	meter (m)
foot (ft)	centimeter (cm)
inch (in.)	millimeter (mm)

AREA

English	Metric
square mile (mi^2)	square kilometer (km^2)
square yard (yd^2)	square meter (m^2)
square foot (ft^2)	square centimeter (cm^2)
square inch (in.^{2})	square millimeter (mm^2)

VOLUME

English	Metric
cubic mile (mi^3)	cubic kilometer (km^3)
cubic yard (yd^3)	cubic meter (m^3)
cubic foot (ft^3)	cubic centimeter (cm^3)
cubic inch (in.^{3})	cubic millimeter (mm^3)
ounce (oz)	liter (L)
	milliliter (mL)

MASS

English	Metric
pound (lb)	kilogram (kg)
ounce (oz)	gram (g)

TIME

hour (hr)

minute (min)

second (s)

FORCE OR WEIGHT

English

ounce (oz)

pound (lb)

Metric

newton (N)

SPEED OR VELOCITY

English

miles per hour (mi/hr)

miles per second (mi/s)

feet per second (ft/s)

Metric

kilometers per hour (km/hr)

kilometers per second (km/s)

meters per second (m/s)

centimeters per second (cm/s)

TEMPERATURE

English

degrees Fahrenheit (°F)

Metric

degrees Celsius (°C)

ENERGY

calorie (cal)

Calorie (Cal)

joule (J)

POWER

watt (W) = joule per second (J/s)

ELECTRICAL UNITS

volt (V)

ampere (A)

MATERIALS

"tin" can lid

6-volt dry cell battery

alligator clips

ammonium chloride (borrow from your science teacher.

balloons

bar magnet

books

cardboard

ceramic disk or rectangular magnets (4 to 6)

clay

clear plastic container

clear plastic tape

cloth, wool and other

coins

copper sheet or screen

copper sulfate (from science teacher or a store that supplies materials for swimming pools)

cork

D-cell (flashlight battery)

drinking glass

enamel-coated wire

flashlight bulb (1.5-volt) such as GE #48

funnel

galvanoscope (made in Activity 11)

glass jar

hammer

insulated copper wire

iron nail

iron filings

knife or wire stripper

lamp

large sewing needle

long stick

long hat pin

magnetic compass

magnets

marking pen

masking tape

measuring tape

milliameter

old metal spoons or carbon rods

paper clips (large and small)

paper

paper towels

pencil

photovoltaic cells (available at a hobby shop or a scientific supply house)

pieces of paper, wood, plastic, rubber

Ping-Pong ball

plastic container

plastic sandwich bag

plastic knitting needle

protractor

ruler

salt

sandpaper

scissors

small test tube or large, clear straw

smooth square board

soft (gray cast) iron rod

spring-type clothespins

steel wool
strong magnet
Styrofoam cup
tacks
test tube
thread
water
wire
zinc sheet

INDEX

ABOUT THE AUTHOR

Robert Gardner, science educator and award-winning author of nonfiction for young people, has written over fifty books to introduce readers to the wonders of science. A *School Library Journal* reviewer has called him "the master of the science experiment book."

He earned a B.A. from Wesleyan University and an M.A. from Trinity College. Before retiring, he taught biology, chemistry, physics, and physical science for over thirty years at Salisbury School in Salisbury, Connecticut. He and his wife, Natalie, reside in Massachusetts where he serves as a consultant on science education and continues to write books for future scientists.